1 2 3 4 5 6 7 8 9 10

Content

3214387777

1 Key messages

- It is time to bring about a fundamental shift in how the NHS is reformed, learning from what has and has not worked in England and elsewhere.

- Politics and policy work on different cycles, which results in short-term political initiatives getting in the way of the long-term policy commitments needed to deliver transformational change.

- Large-scale structural reforms under successive governments have proved a major distraction and should be avoided in future.

- Transforming the NHS depends much less on bold strokes and big gestures by politicians than on engaging doctors, nurses and other staff in improvement programmes.

- A new settlement is needed in which the strategic role of politicians is clearly demarcated to avoid frequent shifts of direction that create barriers to transformational change.

- NHS reform has relied too much on external stimuli such as targets and performance management, inspection and regulation, and competition and choice, and too little on bringing about improvement 'from within'.

- Complementary approaches to reform should be pursued in which national leadership is combined with devolution, collaboration with competition, and innovation with standardisation.

- Devolution and transparency, based on the collection and open reporting of data on performance, should be used more systematically to improve performance.

- Improvement in NHS organisations needs to be based on commitment rather than compliance, supported by investment in staff to enable them to achieve continuous quality improvement in the long as well as the short term.

- The experience of high-performing health care organisations shows the value of leadership continuity, organisational stability, a clear vision and goals for improvement, and the use of an explicit improvement methodology.

- Innovation and experimentation need to be valued more highly in the NHS, with the emerging academic health science networks having a role to play.

- Clinical leadership must be strengthened to promote standardisation of care, with greater emphasis on peer review and peer pressure to improve clinical practice.

- Leadership in NHS organisations needs to be collective and distributed, with skilled clinical leaders working alongside experienced managers, and the role of team leaders given much higher priority.

- NHS organisations need to prioritise leadership development and training in quality improvement methods; this is best done in-house rather than through national agencies.

- Integrated systems are well placed to deliver the innovations in care that are needed through aligning incentives, learning from international exemplars.

Introduction

> *'Philosophers have only interpreted the world in various ways; the point is to change it.'*
> Karl Marx, Theses on Feuerbach, 1845

The aim of this paper is to review different approaches to reforming the NHS in England and to draw out lessons for the future. It focuses on what needs to be done to implement new models of care in the medium and longer term, rather than how to tackle the more immediate financial and service pressures, which has been addressed by other colleagues (Appleby *et al* 2014).

The paper has been written in the context of a growing consensus that current models of health and social care provision are not fit for purpose. The case for fundamental change was set out in an analysis published by The King's Fund (Ham *et al* 2012), and this case has been echoed by NHS England, Monitor and other organisations. There is also a growing consensus that the models of care needed in future should be centred on the following:

- more emphasis on prevention

- support for people to play a bigger part in self-care

- the home as the hub of care, with a wider range of housing options available

- primary care working at scale alongside other services in the community

- less reliance on hospitals and greater concentration of specialist services where the evidence supports this

- much greater integration of care, both within the NHS and between the NHS and other forms of care.

Future models of care have the potential to make much more effective use of information technology (IT) to transform the relationship between service users and providers.

Acknowledging this consensus, there is much less discussion – let alone agreement – on how to move from where we are now to a point in time when these models of care become the reality. This creates a risk, not for the first time, that well-intentioned plans will gather dust on the shelves. To avoid this risk, we have reviewed the impact of different approaches to reform in England, analysed evidence and experience from high-performing health care organisations in other countries, and drawn on research about how companies strive towards excellence and promote innovation. This paper summarises the results of our work in the hope that it will help inform efforts to bring about the transformations in care that are needed. The issues it addresses are becoming increasingly urgent as the financial and service pressures facing the NHS and social care grow, with senior leaders highlighting the consequences of the NHS not embracing change (Campbell 2014a).

The arguments outlined in this paper are as relevant to plans to improve patient safety and quality of care as they are to the implementation of the new models of care described above. At a time when there is increasing awareness of the need to improve safety and quality, there are important choices about how best to do so. These choices include setting targets for the NHS and managing their implementation, making more effective use of the Care Quality Commission (CQC), and collecting and reporting data on the performance of NHS organisations. Another option is to support NHS organisations to develop their own capabilities for improvement. The experience of other countries, as outlined in this paper, offers valuable learning on where the emphasis needs to be placed in the NHS in England in future.

The ideas set out here have been a long time in gestation, and were first sketched in broad outline in a paper for the *British Medical Journal* in 1999 (Ham 1999). In essence, they crystallise my writings and reflections on NHS reform over many years – partly based on experience as a policy-maker and board member of an NHS foundation trust (for example, see chapter 13 in Ham 2009), and as a researcher and evaluator. They also draw on collaborations with colleagues, both within The King's Fund (for example, Ham *et al* 2012) and outside (for example, Bevan *et al* 2008).

My thinking has been strongly shaped by the opportunity to visit, study and learn from health care systems in other countries, which provide a counterpoint in many ways to the NHS. It is for this reason that the paper refers to examples of how other systems have addressed the challenges facing the NHS today in the hope that these will contribute to debate about how the NHS can bring about the transformation in care that is now needed.

③ Three approaches to NHS reform

The NHS has been on a roller-coaster ride of reform for at least 25 years, starting with the internal market introduced by the Thatcher and Major governments, continuing with huge investment and significant reforms under the Blair and Brown governments, and ending (for the time being) with the changes enshrined in the Health and Social Care Act 2012. In this paper we focus on the period from 1997 onwards, which has seen three main approaches to NHS reform, often used in combination: targets and performance management; inspection and regulation; and competition and choice.

Before summarising the impact of these three approaches, it is important to be clear about the problems they were designed to address. Investment and reform under the Blair and Brown governments were intended, in large part, to tackle the long-term underfunding of the NHS and its impacts on patients, which included long waiting times and outcomes that compared poorly with other countries. They were also designed to reduce variations in standards of care and concerns about the so-called postcode lottery in which patients' access to care depended as much on where they lived as on their needs. Other concerns included a health care system that was often unresponsive to the needs of patients and that was slow to innovate.

The Blair government set about tackling these problems by making a commitment to raise spending on health care in England to the European Union average, and linking this spending to the delivery of national standards and targets. This included: establishing the National Institute for Clinical Excellence (NICE) to ensure greater consistency in the funding and provision of drugs and other technologies; publishing a series of national service frameworks setting out standards for the provision of care for people with cancer, heart disease and other conditions; and promulgating targets for improving performance, most visibly in relation to cutting waiting times for treatment. Progress towards meeting standards and targets was reviewed on a regular basis, both within government through a focus on the delivery of public service reform (Barber 2008), and within the NHS through active and often detailed performance management of NHS organisations.

Alongside targets and performance management, the Blair government set up new systems of inspection and regulation within the NHS. This was done by establishing a succession of regulators-cum-inspectors in the form of the Commission for Health Improvement, the Healthcare Commission, and the Care Quality Commission. Their focus was primarily on clinical governance and the quality of care provided by health and (latterly) social care organisations, judged through a combination of visits and inspections, and self-assessment by NHS organisations. Regulators used the results of their assessments to publish information about performance – in part to inform the public and in part to stimulate the organisations being regulated to improve their performance. Through the system of star ratings, and subsequently the annual health check, variations in quality and performance within the NHS became more transparent, with the results being used to identify organisations that needed intervention and support. The 'earned autonomy' regime meant that organisations assessed as performing well received financial bonuses and increased freedom to manage their affairs.

The third main approach to reform during this period – the use of competition and choice – emerged because of concerns within the Blair government that neither targets and performance management nor inspection and regulation were sufficient to bring about the improvements in care needed as a result of the huge increases in investment to which the government was committed. Reversing its commitment to bring an end to the internal NHS market during the 1997 general election, the government designed a much more radical version of provider competition than had been attempted under its Conservative predecessors. Key elements included offering patients a wider choice of provider, introducing the Payment by Results (PbR) funding system to reward hospitals for the work they did, and encouraging much greater plurality of provision through independent sector treatment centres and NHS foundation trusts. These reforms were designed to create stronger incentives to improve performance within the NHS and to reduce reliance on top-down targets and intervention by regulators and inspectors. One of Labour's health secretaries expressed the philosophy behind this approach as being to enable the NHS to become a 'self-improving system' (Hewitt 2006).

It would be wrong to infer that these three approaches to reform were introduced in sequence as part of a logical, well thought through strategy. The reality was much messier and more complex, with all three approaches co-existing from around 2002 onwards in what amounted to an ambitious and far-reaching but not always coherent programme of reform. This presents a challenge for researchers attempting to attribute improvements in NHS care during this period to one or other approach, a challenge compounded by the contribution that increased funding undoubtedly made. With this caveat in mind, what does the evidence suggest about the impact of these three approaches on the NHS?

What impact have these three approaches had?

Various studies have analysed this question, most notably the comprehensive programme of research on New Labour's reforms of the English NHS led by Mays and commissioned by the Department of Health (Mays *et al* 2011). Although primarily about New Labour's market reforms, this programme also examined regulation and system management, and in seeking to evaluate the impact of competition and choice, attempted to understand the influence of other policies pursued at the same time. We have drawn extensively on the findings of this evaluation as well as making use of studies of the internal market in the 1990s (Le Grand *et al* 1998), and other work on targets and performance management (for example, Bevan and Hood 2006), and on inspection and regulation (for example, Walshe 2003). In this section we seek to provide a highly summarised assessment of the verdicts of these studies.

Beginning with targets and performance management, there is clear evidence that this approach contributed to improvements in NHS performance under New Labour. These improvements were most visible in the major reductions in waiting times, but were also apparent in reductions in health care-acquired infections and – through the national service frameworks – improvements in areas of clinical priority like cancer and cardiac care. However, although the targets and performance management approach had positive impacts, there were also some negative consequences. These included evidence of gaming and, in some cases, misreporting of data to avoid penalties and sanctions under the performance management regime. Concerns have also been raised that areas of care not covered by targets may not receive sufficient attention, and that performance management creates a culture of compliance and risk aversion within NHS organisations that inhibits innovation. At its worst, performance management has the effect of disempowering those working in the NHS and creating an over-reliance on central guidance.

Evidence on the impact of inspection and regulation is more difficult to interpret because of frequent changes in the organisations responsible for carrying out this work and in the methods they use. These include routine visits by inspection teams, visits triggered by concerns or analysis of performance data, and self-assessment by NHS organisations using standards developed by regulators. The use of different methods in part reflects uncertainty about the best way of using inspection and regulation to improve quality, and also concern to ensure that they are used proportionately. In his assessment, Bevan (2011) argued that the star rating system used by the regulators in England 'resulted in a transformation of the reported performance of the NHS' (p 105), although it should be noted that the performance referred to encompassed many of the areas of care covered by targets and performance management.

Bevan also notes examples of regulatory failure during this period. These examples concern NHS providers such as Stoke Mandeville Hospital, Maidstone and Tunbridge Wells NHS Trust, and Mid Staffordshire NHS Foundation Trust, where there were serious shortcomings in patient care despite visits by the regulators. In the case of Mid Staffordshire, the Healthcare Commission rated the trust as 'good' in its annual health check in 2007/8 even though it had high standardised mortality ratios. The role of the regulators was one of the issues examined in the two Francis inquiries into the failures of care that occurred at Mid Staffordshire. Major changes have subsequently been implemented in the approach taken by the Care Quality Commission, with the appointment of chief inspectors for hospitals, primary care and social care, and the development and testing of a new regime making use of experts in the areas of care being inspected. The fundamental nature of these changes suggests that inspection and regulation has not yet had the impact that was hoped for when it was introduced in 2000.

The evidence on competition and choice is, in many ways, the most contested. Studies of the internal market in the 1990s concluded that their impact was limited because the incentives were too weak and the constraints too strong (Le Grand *et al* 1998). Foremost among these constraints was an unwillingness on the part of politicians at the time to follow through on the logic of the reforms and allow NHS providers who failed to compete successfully to exit the market – an illustration of the more general point that when politics and markets collide, politics tend to prevail (Ham 2007). The evaluation of New Labour's market reforms similarly concluded that their impact was limited, while also noting that the adverse consequences predicted by opponents of competition and choice had not materialised either.

In an important overall assessment of the impact of different approaches to reform during this period, the leaders of the evaluation observed the following:

> *… many of the gains made before and after 2002/3 were unrelated to competition, patient choice and the rest of the market reform package. Indeed, the predominant narrative on New Labour's period as custodian of the English NHS must focus on the increases in spending and the size of the workforce… after 2000, together with strongly enforced targets, leading to improvements in performance.*
> (Mays *et al* 2011, p 131)

The strongest evidence that competition in the English NHS delivered improvements in performance comes from two econometric studies of the relationship between provider competition and patient outcomes, focusing on death rates in hospitals after heart attack and other causes (Gaynor *et al* 2010; Cooper *et al* 2011). A review of these studies noted that while death rates fell for all hospitals, they fell more rapidly in hospitals located in more competitive markets (Propper and Dixon 2011). What is not clear is whether competition caused this improvement in quality. As the leaders of the evaluation of New Labour's market reforms note in their assessment, it is puzzling that quality should improve for patients with medical conditions that are treated as emergencies when choice of provider is usually not possible. They also note that there may be other reasons why outcomes for these patients improved, including moves to concentrate treatment for some medical conditions in fewer hospitals able to deliver better results (Propper and Dixon 2011).

In relation to patient choice, the most comprehensive study of the impact of New Labour's reforms found that 'the overall impact on the NHS was limited' (Dixon and Robertson 2011, p 63). The reasons for this included patients' loyalty to local NHS providers and the reluctance of GPs to routinely offer patients a choice when making referrals. In deciding where to receive treatment, patients relied heavily on their personal experience, the advice of a trusted professional, and the reputation of a hospital. At the time Dixon and Robertson's study was conducted, convenience and distance were more important considerations in shaping patients' choices than quality of care. There was no evidence that patient choice had an impact on efficiency or provider responsiveness, and overall Dixon and Robertson concluded that 'the evidence summarised here suggests that policy-makers should not rely on patients alone to drive quality improvements' (p 65).

Two other considerations should be borne in mind when assessing the impact of competition and choice in the NHS. The first relates to the transaction costs involved in the market, such as those that arise from contract negotiations between commissioners and providers of care. Even assuming that in some circumstances competition may have a positive impact on the quality of care, the costs associated with achieving this impact may be substantial. The second consideration is the difficulty of designing a market in health care. This encompasses putting in place effective arrangements for market regulation and dealing with provider failure, as well as the political consequences associated with failure alluded to earlier.

It also relates to the continuing challenge in the NHS of ensuring that commissioners can negotiate on equal terms with providers. Commissioners were often described as the 'weak link' in the internal market in the 1990s, and there is no evidence that they were any more effective under New Labour's reforms, notwithstanding ambitious aspirations to achieve 'world class commissioning'. The continuing weakness of commissioners in the NHS can be explained by reference to the complex nature of health care and information asymmetry between providers and commissioners (Ham 2008). This raises questions about how commissioning is organised and resourced, and – more fundamentally – about whether this separation can ever work effectively in health care. We return to these questions in the final section of the paper.

4 Critiques of NHS reform

A critique of the approaches to NHS reform used by New Labour was offered in three independent reviews by US experts in quality improvement, which were commissioned by Lord Darzi when he was health minister during the previous Labour government. The reviews contributed to the NHS next stage review led by Lord Darzi and reported in January 2008, but did not see the light of day until they were released under a Freedom of Information Act request. Undertaken by the Institute for Healthcare Improvement (IHI), the RAND Corporation, and Joint Commission International, the reviews offered a powerful and, in many ways, damning critique of the approach to quality improvement evident in the NHS at that time (Institute for Healthcare Improvement 2008; Joint Commission International 2008; McGlynn *et al* 2008). In doing so, they echoed many of the findings of an audit of the government's record in improving the quality of care in the NHS commissioned by the Nuffield Trust (Leatherman and Sutherland 2008), while expressing concerns about the government's approach in much more critical language.

Key messages included the harmful effects of organisational instability and transient leadership, the existence of a culture of compliance and fear based on targets and performance management, and a gulf between clinicians and managers. One of the reviews (by Joint Commission International) also noted that there were unrealistic expectations about what commissioning could contribute to quality improvement in the NHS, echoing the comments made earlier. The reviews argued that the NHS needed to build a culture of learning and improvement, and to strengthen staff capabilities for improvement. Their core argument was that there had been too much reliance on reforms being led from the top down, and too little on equipping and supporting NHS organisations and staff to lead change and improvement. This included engaging clinicians much more effectively because of their central role in improving patient care.

Although these critiques had some impact on the direction set out by Lord Darzi in the final report of his review, *High quality care for all* (Department of Health 2008), they did not result in a fundamental shift away from the three main approaches to improvement reviewed earlier. Evidence submitted to the Francis public inquiry into Mid Staffordshire NHS Foundation Trust revealed that this was because senior civil servants at the time felt the reviews were superficial in some respects and did not offer a complete or accurate picture of how the government was seeking to improve quality of care (Jarman 2012). Witnesses to the inquiry also argued that some of the recommendations in the reviews were already being acted on, as in the devolution of decision-making to foundation trusts and the intention of the 2012 Health and Social Care Act to limit the powers of the Secretary of State for Health. The one piece of advice contained in the reviews that was embraced with enthusiasm was the argument that clinical leadership and engagement should be strengthened, perhaps not surprisingly in view of Lord Darzi's own background as a surgeon.

The challenge under successive governments has been to put into practice the apparent commitment to devolution and to restricting the role of politicians in NHS reform. Successive secretaries of state for health talked of 'shifting the balance of power in the NHS' (Alan Milburn in 2001), the NHS becoming a 'self-improving organisation' (Patricia Hewitt in 2006), and 'liberating' the NHS (Andrew Lansley in 2010), which all seemed to herald a new dawn; but the reality has been quite different. Regardless of which political party is in government, there appears to be an irresistible tendency for ministers to want to be seen to be leading the NHS, driven by intense media scrutiny and the Secretary of State's ultimate accountability for the performance of the NHS. The positive impact of targets and performance management in bringing about improvements in care reinforces the tendency of politicians to revert to this approach when they are under pressure.

At the time of writing, funding and service pressures in the NHS have resulted in ministers being as closely involved in overseeing performance as ever. This is despite the intentions of those who framed the 2012 Act to limit the powers of the health secretary, and commitments given after the 2010 general election to focus on outcomes rather than targets. Ministers have also acted to strengthen inspection and regulation through the Care Quality Commission (CQC) following the second Francis inquiry and evidence of failures of patient care at a number of NHS hospitals that have been placed in special measures. As a consequence, the coalition government has extended many of the policies put in place by New Labour, including those on competition and choice, and the negative consequences of some of these policies continue to be felt. The result is a set of reforms that are even more complex than those they replaced (Gregory *et al* 2012).

The negative consequences of the reforms pursued by successive governments have been highlighted by Seddon (2008) in his critique of command-and-control thinking in public sector reform. He contrasts this way of thinking with systems thinking, drawing on the work of Deming (whose influence on performance improvement in health care is outlined in the box below) and the application of this work in companies like Toyota (*see* Figure 1). Systems thinking underpins the approach to quality improvement in health care taken by the IHI, and there are therefore strong parallels between its critique of New Labour's approach to NHS reform and Seddon's analysis of the weaknesses of command-and-control thinking. Both the IHI and Seddon express a preference for reforms that appeal to the intrinsic motivation of staff providing public services to lead improvements in performance, linked to a belief that sustainable improvements depend on building commitment to change rather than seeking compliance with externally imposed targets and standards. This approach seeks to move away from using external stimuli to bring about performance improvements towards supporting NHS organisations and staff to lead and deliver improvements.

Edwards Deming

A theme running through this report is the impact of Dr W Edwards Deming's thinking on quality improvement in health care. Deming was an American whose theory of management influenced Japanese industry after the second world war and subsequently shaped thinking in a wide range of sectors, including health care, in other countries. He was critical of the role of inspection in improving quality and emphasised instead the importance of leadership and measurement. He argued that quality should be built into production from the outset and that the focus should be on the system of production and how this contributed to quality. His thinking lies behind the use of plan–do–study–act to test out improvements in health care, and he was a powerful advocate of continuous improvement. His writings have been brought together in an edited collection by Orsini (2013).

Figure 1 Command-and-control versus systems thinking

Command-and-control thinking		Systems thinking
Top-down, hierarchy	**Perspective**	Outside-in, system
Functional	**Design**	Demand, value and flow
Separated from work	**Design-making**	Integrated with work
Output, targets, standards: related to budget	**Measurement**	Capability, variation: related to purpose
Contractual	**Attitude to customers**	What matters?
Contractual	**Attitude to suppliers**	Co-operative
Manage people and budgets	**Role of management**	Act on the system
Control	**Ethos**	Learning
Reactive, projects	**Change**	Adaptive, integral
Extrinsic	**Motivation**	Intrinsic

Source: Seddon 2008

This perspective has not been ignored in recent approaches to public service reform in England, and indeed was identified as one of the main ways of improving public services in a review by the Cabinet Office in 2006 (*see* Figure 2). In the case of the NHS, the work of the NHS Modernisation Agency between 2001 and 2005 is perhaps the best example of a concerted attempt to adapt learning from the IHI and similar organisations, as well as drawing on expertise within the NHS. The Agency grew out of the National Patients' Access Team, which had achieved some success in supporting the NHS to reduce waiting times, and a number of other improvement initiatives (Timmins and Gash 2014). The Agency's work focused initially on the implementation of the booked appointments system, the cancer services collaborative, and a programme to reduce waiting times in accident and emergency (A&E) departments. It also contributed to the development of skills in quality improvement and service redesign – for example, in work to improve access in A&E departments. From small beginnings, it expanded to take on many more improvement programmes, and by 2003 employed 800 staff. In effect, it became an agent of government rather than an expert body working alongside NHS organisations and supporting them to improve care.

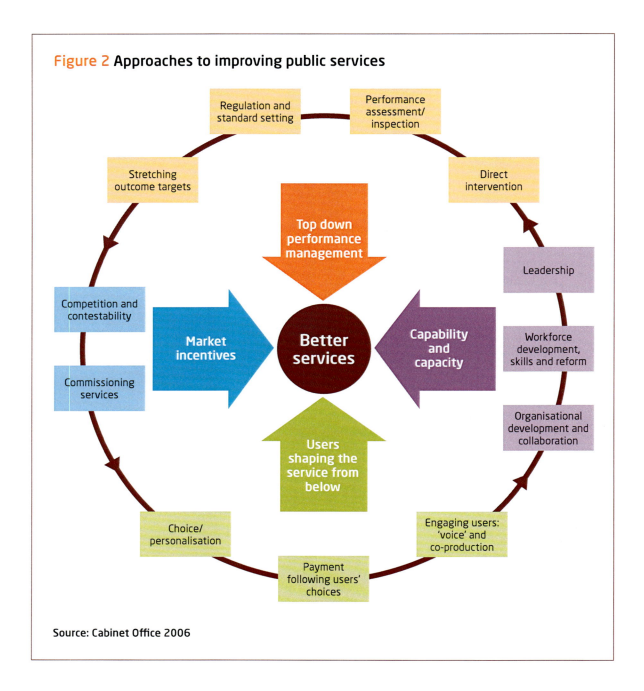

Figure 2 Approaches to improving public services

Source: Cabinet Office 2006

The rapid growth of the NHS Modernisation Agency was testament to its success, but also created problems. These included staff with improvement expertise being taken away from work in NHS organisations directly providing patient care to work on national programmes set up to support and advise these organisations on how to achieve improvements. NHS organisations found themselves receiving support from more than one of the national programmes being run by the Agency, often with weak co-ordination between them. These and other factors led to a decision to wind down the Agency's work; greater emphasis was to be placed on improvement programmes being led at regional and local levels, with national expertise concentrated in a smaller national body, the NHS Institute for Innovation and Improvement. Its former chief executive is now leading a regional agency established from within the NHS in the north-west of England to provide support on quality and service improvement (Timmins and Gash 2014). An assessment of the impact of the Agency's work, conducted by its own staff and independent researchers, identified a number of successes and challenges in spreading innovations and improvements in care between organisations (Buchanan *et al* 2007).

Reforming health care from within

Despite the mixed record of the NHS Modernisation Agency, its experience points to a key lesson about health care reform – namely, the importance of bringing about change and improvement 'from within' by investing in staff and appealing to their intrinsic motivation to provide the best possible care within available resources. This lesson derives from two sources: first, the known limits to reforms that depend on external stimuli such as targets and performance management, inspection and regulation, and competition and choice; and second, the experience of high-performing organisations (*see* below). As one commentator who was at the heart of New Labour's reforms of public services observed (of targets and performance management), this approach may be appropriate when performance is poor and needs to be improved, but it is not likely to be sufficient when the aim is to transform performance from adequate or good to great (Barber 2008), which is precisely what is required of the NHS today.

The experience of high-performing health care organisations in other countries offers a radically different perspective to the journey of reform undertaken by the NHS (Baker *et al* 2008). As research has shown, high-performing organisations have often pursued quite different routes to improvement (Bate *et al* 2008), and they have certainly not been able to escape the impact of inspection and regulation, competition and choice, and other external stimuli. However, their experience illustrates the value of a sustained commitment to quality improvement based on clarity of goals and systematic measurement of progress towards them. This has often been underpinned by an explicit methodology for bringing about quality improvement, and the provision of training, development and support for staff to enable them to improve care. These organisations have benefited from continuity of leadership, and they have avoided the frequent organisational changes that have been so damaging to the NHS.

Examples of high-performing organisations making improvements from within

Below are four examples from different parts of the world and one from the NHS in England, which shed greater light on these insights.

Jönköping County Council in Sweden is an elected regional health authority serving a population of around 330,000 and is widely recognised for the high-quality care it provides. Over a period of 20 years, it has pursued a population-based vision of 'a good life in an attractive county'. This includes achieving strong financial performance and a commitment to continuous quality improvement in the delivery of health and social care. Its work has been informed by a concern to deliver the best possible outcomes for 'Esther', a fictional older resident whose experience was used to enable clinical staff to map care pathways and explore how they could be improved to better meet Esther's needs.

County councils in Sweden have considerable autonomy by virtue of the devolved system of government in that country and their tax-raising powers. Jönköping's work on quality improvement initially benefited from involvement with the Institute for Healthcare Improvement (IHI) in the Pursuing Perfection programme. Through this programme, leaders adopted a methodology for quality improvement and applied this to services in the county's 3 hospitals and 34 primary care centres. The relationship with IHI was formed through contact from the top leadership team and was progressively extended to staff throughout the organisation.

Building on this experience, Jönköping established its own in-house centre for learning and improvement known as Qulturum. This centre delivers education, training and learning in quality improvement to the county council's staff, drawing on links with international experts such as Don Berwick and Paul Batalden. Thousands of staff have taken part in the programmes run at Qulturum as an expression of the council's commitment not only to quality improvement but also to becoming a learning organisation. The results of this work over many years are evident, as Jönköping compares favourably with other county councils on measures of quality of care in national rankings.

Intermountain Healthcare is a non-profit health care system in the United States, employing 32,000 staff in 23 hospitals and 160 clinics and primary care centres. Whereas Jönköping adopted a population-based vision for improvement, starting in 1986 Intermountain aimed to promote clinical excellence through the systematic pursuit of evidence-based medicine. It did so by measuring variations in clinical practice, feeding the results back to the clinicians concerned, and working with clinicians to develop guidelines and protocols for improving care, drawing on available evidence. Importantly, improvement occurs in part by allowing exceptions to guidelines, and using these to learn how care can be strengthened.

As in Jönköping, Intermountain's work is underpinned by a long-term commitment to quality improvement, and a substantial investment in training and learning through its own Advanced Training Programme. This programme was developed by the Chief Quality Officer, Brent James, who had a background in mathematics and engineering, and involves a four-week commitment from participants, who include clinicians and managers. The curriculum includes the development of leadership skills and also training in quality improvement methods and statistical techniques drawing on the work of Deming and others. Participants are required to apply their learning in a practical project before they graduate from the programme.

The impressive improvements in quality that have occurred at Intermountain have resulted from a relentless focus on tackling variations and reducing waste in clinical practices. Many areas of care have benefited, ranging from intensive care to primary care. More than almost any other high-performing organisation, Intermountain has succeeded in standardising care around accepted good practice, and its experience (confirming Deming's view) indicates that high-quality care often costs less. One example is its work on substantially reducing mortality from infections of the blood, thereby setting a new national standard (Gomez 2010).

This and other work is supported by an investment in real-time information systems and a culture in which staff achieve improvements through a commitment to providing the best possible care rather than by having to comply with an externally imposed standard. James (personal communication) contrasts Deming's philosophy with Taylorism, arguing that change driven from the top down is much less effective and sustainable than change that arises from the bottom up. The aim is to 'make the right thing the easy thing to do' by ensuring that the default position for physicians is the best practice standard agreed by leaders of clinical programmes. An example of Intermountain's approach is described later.

Canterbury District Health Board (DHB) in New Zealand has focused its quality improvement work on integrating health and social care to tackle growing demands for hospital care for an ageing population. The DHB serves just over 500,000 people and delivers care through 9,000 staff employed across a range of hospital, community, and primary care providers. While working within a framework set by the Minister of Health in Wellington, the DHB has greater freedom than is typically available to NHS organisations to use its resources (allocated by the Ministry of Health) to improve health and care. The majority of its members are elected locally, with a minority appointed by the minister.

The focus on integrating health and social care arose out of concern that increased hospital capacity would be needed unless action was taken to stem growing demands for hospital care, which would be unaffordable. The DHB's leaders responded to this concern by developing a vision for the future based on the notion that there was 'one system, one budget', and that all those involved in the system needed to work together to improve care. This resulted in a commitment to build on the strengths of primary care in Canterbury and, particularly, to invest in services that would help avoid hospital admissions and facilitate early discharge where appropriate. These and many other initiatives enabled the DHB to stem the increase in hospital use. They also helped the system cope with the effects of the 2011 earthquakes that destroyed some of the hospital capacity in Christchurch.

These results were achieved through sustained investment in providing staff and organisations under contract with the DHB with the skills needed to improve care and develop innovative models of provision. This was done by providing training in quality improvement methods such as Lean and Six Sigma, and arranging visits to other organisations that had used these methods such as Air New Zealand and New Zealand Post. More than 1,000 staff from across the DHB took part in this training, which had the effect of building momentum and commitment to the changes that were needed. Experts in process engineering were also used to support clinicians and managers to redesign care pathways and work flows in order to cut waste and improve performance (Timmins and Ham 2013).

The journey of improvement in Canterbury, as in the other examples described here, benefited from organisational stability and leadership continuity. It also benefited from collective leadership across the system based on the involvement of very many people at all levels. The DHB's achievements were recognised in a report from the New Zealand Auditor-General in 2013, which rated Canterbury's management control for the previous financial year as 'very good' – one of only two district health boards to receive this top rating. Its financial information systems were described as good (no other health board did better), while Canterbury became the only health board, and one of only 4 per cent of all New Zealand public bodies, to be judged to have 'very good' service performance information.

The Virginia Mason Medical Center in Seattle is the fourth example of a high-performing health care organisation that illustrates how improvement can be achieved from within. Recognising the need to improve patient safety and the quality of care, Virginia Mason's leaders visited Japan in 2001 to learn about the Toyota Production System (TPS). On their return to Seattle, they began to develop the Virginia Mason Production System (VMPS). This draws directly on Deming's systems thinking and particularly the elimination of waste. It does so through the systematic use of a management method in which the patient is put first, and sources of waste are identified and eliminated over time through value stream mapping and other techniques.

The VMPS would not have happened without the initial commitment of the organisation's top leaders and it would not have become embedded and sustained without the involvement of staff throughout the organisation. Crucially, many hundreds of staff were trained in methods of quality improvement in which there was a strong focus on identifying and tackling variations in care and developing 'standard work' (Kenney 2010). While the use of a management method was fundamental to this approach, it was combined with leadership commitment, rigour, and the discipline to stick the course even in the face of setbacks. Not least, the emphasis on standard work ran up against the prized autonomy of physicians, meaning that in some cases physicians chose to leave the Medical Center to work elsewhere.

The fact that only a few physicians left reflects the effort put into alignment between physicians and the leaders of the Medical Center, assisted by the development of an explicit compact early on in the journey (Kenney 2010). It also reflects the organisation's investment in staff training and development, including equipping them with the quality improvement skills needed to improve care processes. This involves rapid process improvement workshops in which staff use the management method developed within the VMPS to 'define the existing process; establish measures and targets; observe, measure, and critique the existing process; develop and experiment with an improved process; and implement' (Bohmer 2009, p 211).

Commentators on the VMPS have argued that one of the advantages enjoyed by the Medical Center in undertaking this work was its structure – that is, being a large integrated delivery system working with an exclusively affiliated and salaried medical group. This, together with a cohesive culture, meant that it had or was able to develop the capabilities needed to bring about change (Pham *et al* 2007). Having made this point, there is an interesting contrast with Intermountain Healthcare – also an integrated delivery system but with a large group of independent community-based practitioners as well as its own physician group.

James and Savitz note that in Intermountain, this meant 'We didn't try to control physicians' practice behaviour by top-down command and control through an employment relationship. Instead we relied on solid process and outcome data, professional values that focused on patients' needs, and a shared culture of high quality' (James and Savitz 2011, p 1189). This suggests that culture is more important than structure in bringing about improvements in care – perhaps not surprisingly in organisations where those delivering care are skilful and often autonomous professionals, regardless of their formal employment status.

An example from within the NHS

Closer to home, Salford Royal NHS Foundation Trust is one of a growing number of NHS organisations that share some of the characteristics found in these international examples. The trust is widely acknowledged to be a high-performing organisation, and has one of the highest levels of patient satisfaction. These results are underpinned by consistently good performance in the annual NHS staff survey. The trust has benefited from continuity of leadership and consistent pursuit of its vision to be a safe and high-quality provider of care.

Salford's journey of improvement began in 2007 when one of its senior leaders spent time at the IHI in Boston and learned about its work on patient safety and quality improvement. On her return, the trust developed its first quality improvement strategy, with the ambitious aim of becoming the safest organisation within the

NHS. The strategy evolved over time in the light of experience, with the key goals being to reduce mortality, improve patient experience, reduce harm, and improve reliability (*see* Figure 3).

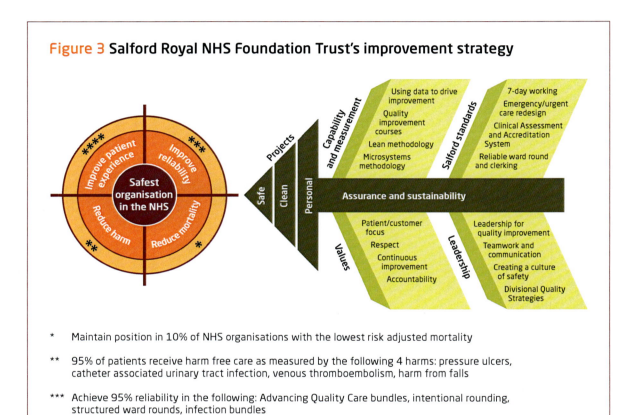

Figure 3 Salford Royal NHS Foundation Trust's improvement strategy

*   Maintain position in 10% of NHS organisations with the lowest risk adjusted mortality

**   95% of patients receive harm free care as measured by the following 4 harms: pressure ulcers, catheter associated urinary tract infection, venous thromboembolism, harm from falls

***   Achieve 95% reliability in the following: Advancing Quality Care bundles, intentional rounding, structured ward rounds, infection bundles

**** Achieve top 20% for patient and staff experience surveys

Source: Salford Royal NHS Foundation Trust 2013. Salford Royal is happy to grant The King's Fund the right to use in print or electronic form, the diagrammatic figure from its publication, *Quality Accounts 2012–2013*, section 2, p 8; G13041505 Design Services, Salford Royal NHS Foundation Trust, published June 2013.

These goals have been pursued by developing a culture focused on delivering safe care (in fact, the watchwords at the trust are 'safe, clean and personal'). The culture embraces a number of values that staff are expected to exhibit – namely, being patient- and customer-focused, supportive of continuous improvement, respectful, and accountable. Staff are supported to put these values into practice through training and development, much of which is delivered in-house. The content includes improvement skills, understanding of Lean methods and tools, and statistical measurement. These skills are then applied in a rolling programme of quality improvement projects.

During its improvement journey, the trust changed the way it organised its work to create four clinical divisions, each headed by a clinical chair supported by a managing director and nursing director. Responsibility for budgets and services was devolved to these divisions, and unusually, there is no director of operations on the executive team. There were significant investments in developing medical leaders to ensure that clinical chairs and clinical directors had the skills needed to operate in the new structure. This included developing an explicit compact with medical staff, drawing on the work of Jack Silversin (Edwards *et al* 2002).

Members of the executive team are associated with each of the divisions, but as coaches and advisors rather than managers. Executive team members play their part in implementing the quality improvement strategy through safety walkarounds and by spending time at the 'front line'. The trust board monitors progress on the strategy through regular performance reports, revising goals for improvement as necessary. Use of the patient safety thermometer enables the board to track progress in reducing incidents of harm.

The other main strand of work that Salford Royal embarked on involved seeking to achieve greater alignment between the trust's strategy and the contribution of the 6,500 staff who work for the organisation. This has benefited from a partnership with GE and the adaptation of GE's approach to objective setting and appraisals, with a focus on values and behaviours. This has been challenging – not least for medical staff – but is seen by the chief executive as fundamentally important in taking quality improvement to the next level by engaging all staff in delivering the organisation's objectives. Good performance is rewarded, with pay progression dependent on the outcome of appraisals.

The results of this work include Salford being in the top 10 per cent of NHS organisations on risk adjusted mortality, and receiving the highest staff satisfaction/ engagement rating of any acute trust for three consecutive years. Over 90 per cent of patients rate their care as 'excellent' or 'very good'. Other specific achievements include substantial reductions in rates of pressure ulcers, catheter associated urinary tract infections, and orthopaedic surgical site infections. Put more positively, over 97 per cent of patients receive harm-free care (Salford Royal NHS Foundation Trust 2013).

The learning organisation

In their different ways, the examples of high-performing health care organisations we have described illustrate what it means to be a learning organisation committed to delivering continuous improvements in care. By focusing on bringing about improvement from within, they have developed the capability to review current practices and have been able to adapt their strategies in the light of experience. Often, this has been done by tackling variations, reducing waste and seeking to standardise how care is delivered; these efforts have been supported by measurement and the use of quality improvement methods informed by systems thinking, particularly the influential work of Deming and others who have drawn on his seminal work. Learning organisations such as those we have described share a commitment to high reliability and to providing the best possible care within the resources available.

Their experience has contributed to a comprehensive analysis of the essential characteristics of a learning health care system by the Institute of Medicine (IOM) in the United States (*see* Figure 4). These characteristics include science and informatics, patient–clinician partnerships, incentives, and culture – all aligned to promote and enable continuous and real-time improvement in both the effectiveness and efficiency of care. As the IOM notes, there are major challenges in implementing this vision in real-world clinical environments, and these will not be overcome through incremental changes. Rather, a system-wide approach is needed, acting on several fronts at the same time. This may explain why there are relatively few examples of high-performing organisations that also have the characteristics of a learning health care system.

One of the insights from high-performing and high-reliability organisations is the sheer time it takes to bring about transformational change in health care. The organisations we have described have been on a long-term journey of improvement, often extending over 20–30 years. This reflects the obstacles that have to be overcome and the effort that needs to be applied, rather than any lack of urgency on their part. Importantly, as Chassin and Loeb have observed from experience in the United States, 'the primary drive for change must ultimately come from the health care organisations themselves' (Chassin and Loeb 2013, p 484) rather than from regulators or legislators. They go on to add: 'One of the most important roles for policy-makers and stakeholders is to encourage, persuade, and demand that health care organizations embark on this journey. Even after they have committed to do so, how long it will take for health care organizations to reach high reliability is unknown' (ibid).

To make this point is to emphasise that bringing about change and improvement 'from within' is not an easy path to take. All of the organisations described here have made a sustained and long-term commitment to quality and service improvement in which their leaders have been deeply involved from the outset. These leaders have shown the way by being visibly committed to improving care and understanding the need to work with and through many hundreds of staff to achieve results. In the process, they have demonstrated resilience in overcoming barriers to improvement, and often scepticism from some of the staff affected by change. None would claim that the journey of improvement they have embarked on is complete, and all recognise that without constant vigilance, there is the risk that performance may slip back.

Figure 4 Characteristics of a continuously learning health care system

Science and informatics	**Real-time access to knowledge** A learning health care system continuously and reliably captures, curates and delivers the best available evidence to guide, support, tailor and improve clinical decision making and care safety and quality.
	Digital capture of the care experience A learning health care system captures the care experience on digital platforms for real-time generation and application of knowledge for care improvement.
Patient–clinician partnerships	**Engaged, empowered patients** A learning health care system is anchored on patient needs and perspectives and promotes the inclusion of patients, families and other caregivers as vital members of the continuously learning care team.
Incentives	**Incentives aligned for value** A learning health care system has incentives actively aligned to encourage continuous improvement, identify and reduce waste and reward high-value care.
	Full transparency A learning health care system systematically monitors the safety, quality, processes, prices, costs and outcomes of care and makes information available for care improvement and informed choices and decision making by clinicians, patients and their families.
Continuous learning culture	**Leadership-instilled culture of learning** A learning health care system is stewarded by leadership committed to a culture of teamwork, collaboration and adaptability in support of continuous learning as a core aim.
	Supportive system competencies A learning health care system constantly refines complex care operations and processes through ongoing team training and skill building, systems analysis and information development and creation of the feedback loops for continuous learning and system development.

Source: Smith *et al* 2013

6 Complementary approaches to reform

The limited impact of reforms that rely on external stimuli, and the experience of high-performing health care organisations that bring about improvement from within, raise important questions about the means that should be used in the NHS to migrate towards the new models of care described at the beginning of this paper. These questions take on added force because it is unlikely that there will be real-terms increases in the NHS budget in the short to medium term, which means it will not have the additional investment that contributed significantly to improvements in performance in the 2000s. Our conclusions on the limited impact of external stimuli are strongly reinforced in a new analysis by Bevan *et al* (2014) of the performance of the NHS in England, Northern Ireland, Scotland and Wales, which found that broadly similar results have been achieved despite different approaches to reform.

The experience of high-performing organisations in other countries provides powerful evidence of what NHS organisations themselves can do to transform how care is delivered. The unanswered question is what approach should be taken by those leading the NHS at a national level to support NHS organisations locally in this task, and to facilitate change across the NHS *as a system*? More specifically (and because not all leaders will have the vision or capabilities evident in the examples described earlier), what approach is most likely to enable the NHS as a whole to make the transformational changes that are needed to ensure its sustainability?

An example that offers an instructive parallel with the challenges facing the NHS in England today is the Veterans Health Administration (VA), which underwent a fundamental transformation in the second half of the 1990s. Under new leadership, the VA was transformed from an inefficient and unresponsive public health care system to an organisation that was widely admired for its ability to provide high-quality care at an affordable cost to the people it served. This involved migrating from a fragmented, hospital-centred system to a series of regionally based integrated service networks, and in the process reducing the use of hospitals and strengthening out-of-hospital services.

Studies show that the quality of care in the VA improved measurably as a result of these and other changes, and it has been held up as an example for other health systems to learn from and emulate (Asch *et al* 2004). Of critical importance in the VA, and of particular relevance to the NHS today, was the willingness of its national leaders to support network directors in closing hospitals where appropriate in order to release resources for reinvestment in services in the community, even in the face of opposition from politicians. Also relevant was the VA's focus during this transformation on improving patient safety and quality of care, particularly as these issues become more salient for the NHS.

For our purposes, the main learning from the VA's experience relates to how improvement was achieved. In brief, over a period of five years, it took a number of inter-related actions, including agreeing a new vision, implementing an organisational structure (in the form of integrated service networks) to achieve this vision, and appointing the right people to make it happen. Oliver (2007), among others, has distilled the following factors as being important in the turnaround of the VA.

- The introduction of a performance management approach, setting out measurable goals for improving quality and outcomes.

- The use of performance contracts agreed between the VA's leaders and network directors.

- The development of a culture of measurement and reporting at all levels to support performance management.

- The devolution of responsibility for implementing goals to managers at different levels, in place of the previous system of micromanagement.

- The use of financial and non-financial incentives to support quality improvement, including transparent reporting of comparative performance.

- The use of information technology to support integration of care.

- Investment in health services research and evaluation as part of a culture of learning and improvement.

- The strengthening of leadership at all levels.

In describing the transformation that occurred, Kizer and Dudley (2009) note how the unreformed VA exhibited 'a fault-finding, untrusting, punitive culture in response to its command and control, military-style management, and the organization's intense oversight by Congress…'. This meant that much of the operational decision-making was centralised in the VA's headquarters, resulting in slow decision-making and increased politicisation of issues. Over time, this was replaced with much greater delegation of decision-making to network directors, in which 'The goal was to decentralize decision making to the lowest, most appropriate management level and then to hold management accountable for their decisions'.

The VA story shows the importance of clinical leadership and the value of investing in staff and providing them with the skills and capabilities to bring about change and improvement. Clinicians were engaged by focusing the change programme on patient safety, quality of care and outcomes, rather than financial performance and efficiency, on the basis that this would resonate more effectively with them. Clinical leaders were also supported by investment in information systems that provided them with the data needed to both manage operations and bring about improvements in care. As in the examples cited earlier, a key priority was to standardise care around best practice in order to reduce the wide and unacceptable variations in quality that previously pervaded the VA.

The experience of the VA also validates Pettigrew's argument that transformational change in complex organisations involves moving beyond simple dichotomies such as top-down vs bottom-up by explicitly recognising the need for **complementary approaches** to bringing about change (Pettigrew 1999). Pettigrew's writings on complementary approaches to change grew out of studies of how high-performing companies undertook transformations, but as the VA's experience shows, there are striking parallels with health care. The VA's story shows the importance of setting a clear direction for the organisation as a whole while devolving responsibility for implementation to directors of integrated service networks. Network directors competed with each other to improve performance while also collaborating and sharing learning across the system. One of the most important complementary changes was to ensure continuity of service delivery during the transformation while implementing extensive innovation in all aspects of the VA system at a rapid pace, reflecting the urgency facing the system at the time.

Many of these points about the process of reform are echoed in Leatherman and Sutherland's critique of New Labour's quality strategy, in which they argued for greater consistency, avoidance of multiple overlapping initiatives, and 'moving away from swings between centrally-driven and patchy locally-driven change towards a refined and stable reform agenda that recognises and builds upon the nationalised health system properties of the NHS' (Leatherman and Sutherland 2008, p xiv). They added that there was a need to progress beyond the rift between central control of the NHS and devolution to local levels and recognise the role of agencies across a continuum 'so that initiatives appropriate for central push are identified alongside those that need more definition from local levels to co-exist harmoniously' (p 17). This is precisely the rationale for complementary approaches to change, and it underlines the continuing role for central leadership alongside local ownership of quality improvement programmes.

The NHS also has much to learn from the VA in relation to its operating structure and funding system. Change on the scale that occurred would not have been possible without the establishment of integrated service networks funded through capitated budgets. Network directors were able to reshape service provision, which involved reducing the use of hospital beds by over 50 per cent and reinvesting the savings in primary care and care in community settings. The danger of integrated service networks becoming unresponsive monopolies in their regions was addressed through measuring and reporting on their performance, and through the internal competition that was generated between network directors. Initially, this was driven by central direction, but subsequently this gave way to regional leadership, with network directors having much greater autonomy than their predecessors to bring about change. Decentralisation of decision-making unleashed innovation on a scale not seen before, but it also created problems because of the speed at which it happened and the lack of capability among some leaders (Young 2000).

Learning from the VA, as well as from experience in devolved health care systems in New Zealand and Sweden, much more could be done to measure and report openly on the performance of NHS organisations as a way of supporting quality improvement. In the VA, network directors met regularly with the VA's national leaders to review performance on key indicators. They were challenged by their peers in a system where there was internal competition to perform well and to be seen to be doing so. A similar approach contributed to improvements in the performance of the police service in New York, where precinct commanders reviewed weekly crime data on a precinct-by-precinct basis (Kelling and Bratton 1998). In both examples, there was reputational damage for leaders whose performance lagged behind that of others.

This approach is also used in Sweden, where county councils are the main organisations responsible for funding and providing health care services in a devolved, publicly funded system. Their performance is assessed on a number of criteria and the results are published to support improvement. Equally important is the long-established use of disease registries in Sweden – almost 90 in total – which collect data from providers and make these publicly available. Analysis shows that by focusing on collecting and reporting accurate information, with the active engagement of the clinical community, disease registries have contributed to improvements in outcomes (Larsson *et al* 2012).

A final observation on the VA is that it has experienced major challenges in holding onto the gains made during its transformation. Recently these challenges have included lengthening waiting times for treatment and concerns about variable quality of care, resulting in a change of leadership. This is an important reminder that the journey to high performance is rarely linear and never one way. It does not, however, invalidate the lessons identified above from its remarkable transformation in the 1990s.

Innovation and standardisation

One of the most important complementary changes the NHS needs to embrace is to encourage innovation and experimentation on the one hand, while supporting efforts to standardise care on the other. Innovation and experimentation are crucial because, at a time of constrained resources, it is essential that the inertia that often characterises health care systems is challenged (Coiera 2011). Inertia results from institutional complexity as well as professional autonomy, with different countries following their own 'logics' of reform as described by Tuohy in her comparative analysis (Tuohy 1999). This explains why incremental adjustment is the usual outcome of reform even when politicians pursue 'big bang' strategies.

Harford's analysis of innovation in different sectors emphasises the value of embracing mistakes and the ability to learn from them because 'success always starts with failure' (Harford 2001). His work challenges the view that centralised control, based on great leaders who gather more and more information to ensure effective implementation of their plans, will work. Evidence from recent military conflicts and attempts at centralised economic planning shows the folly of such an approach. The same evidence demonstrates the value of allowing military commanders on the ground the flexibility to adapt plans in the light of experience, using feedback to change course as necessary. The more general point to emerge from Harford's critique is the value of experimentation and trial and error. The challenge then is to survive failures by recognising when they have occurred and containing the consequences.

In a complex adaptive system like the NHS, innovation is unlikely to be promoted through conventional linear change models that rely on leadership from the top. Rather, it depends on fostering networks through which ideas and practices can spread, making use of the emerging academic health science centres and networks and other means. One promising example is the UCLPartners Academic Health Science Partnership, which was established in 2009 by a university and four teaching hospitals. It has subsequently expanded to cover 6 million people in parts of London, Essex, Hertfordshire and Bedfordshire.

UCLPartners is a partnership of autonomous health care providers and higher education institutions with a shared vision of delivering high-value health care. Thematic directors work across the partners and provide leadership through influence and support. Achievements to date include: the establishment of an integrated cancer system known as London Cancer serving 3.2 million people, with the aim of improving outcomes for people with 11 different types of tumours; and the Deteriorating Patient Collaborative designed to reduce avoidable cardiac arrests by 50 per cent. The latter began as a collaboration of six trusts in north-central London and currently encompasses 15 trusts.

These initiatives build on an earlier programme on stroke care, which was part of a London-wide plan to concentrate hyperacute stroke services in eight hospitals in the capital in place of the 34 hospitals that were previously providing care. All units that wished to provide these services submitted a bid to an expert panel of clinicians from outside London, and successful sites were selected on the basis of quality, performance, geographic fit (to ensure adequate coverage and provision across London) and other criteria. The new model of stroke care was implemented after a lengthy period of evidence gathering and consensus building. Evaluation has shown that it has delivered improved outcomes, and costs were saved within two years of implementation (Hunter *et al* 2013).

These and other examples lend support to Atul Gawande's argument that spreading innovations, pace Everett Rogers, is essentially a social process that hinges on effective person-to-person communication rather than technological solutions or indeed the use of incentives and penalties (Gawande 2013). If, as he contends, people follow the example of those they know and trust, then there is no alternative to creating time and opportunities for credible leaders and innovators to offer time and support to those seeking to bring about improvements in care. There are some examples of this within the NHS – for instance, the use of learning collaboratives and agencies like the Emergency Care Intensive Support Team in England (ECIST), which provides assistance to organisations seeking to improve the performance of their emergency and urgent care services. But more initiatives are needed to accelerate reform from within.

At a time of constrained resources, many innovations depend on existing services being decommissioned in order to fund new services to take their place. There is valuable learning here from the transformation of mental health services over the past 40 years, which has involved a major shift away from care in the former asylums to most services being based in the community. A recent review by The King's Fund distilled the successes and failures of this programme, including the importance of investing in new capacity before existing capacity is closed, and of allowing for double running costs during the period of transition. Equally important was to redesign the service model, instead of simply providing the same services in new settings. Underpinning these changes was strategic planning and leadership by regional health authorities, and supporting staff through training and the use of improvement methodologies (Gilburt *et al* 2014).

Supporting experimentation and innovation does not mean that system leaders should abdicate their responsibilities; as Harford emphasises, 'the correct balance between centralised control and decentralised experimentation depends on circumstance' (2001, p 227). In a nuclear power station, for example, it would be dangerous to encourage engineers to experiment with new ways of running the reactor. Likewise, in an NHS hospital, it would be harmful and unsafe for surgeons to test new procedures where there is evidence and professional consensus on the most appropriate way of treating patients with specific conditions. The example of stroke care in London, discussed above, is a case in point, illustrating the value of centralising specialist services in fewer hospitals.

The stroke care example also shows why standardisation of care is needed, across many different areas, to ensure delivery of the highest-quality care within available resources. As the case studies of high-performing health care organisations described earlier show, quality improvement depends on identifying and reducing unwarranted variations in clinical practice patterns. Where this has been done, quality has improved and savings have been made, as in the example from Intermountain Healthcare (*see* box below).

How Intermountain Healthcare tackled unwarranted variations in clinical practice

The experience of Intermountain Healthcare holds important learning for the NHS on tackling unwarranted variations in clinical practice patterns. An early example was its work to measure variations among surgeons treating prostate cancer. This involved analysing, for each surgeon, the time taken to operate, the amount of tissue extracted, the costs of each procedure, and the outcomes. The results showed wide differences which, when fed back to the surgeons, led to agreement on a new guideline for treatment. Over time, this not only reduced variations in surgical practice but also cut costs and, most importantly, improved outcomes (see www.kingsfund.org.uk/audio-video/brent-james-achieving-transformational-change-how-become-high-performing-organisation).

A similar method was applied to other areas of care, with the doctors concerned taking responsibility for bringing about improvements through a combination of measurement of variation, the development of guidelines, and peer monitoring and review. Intermountain focused on 104 medical conditions that accounted for around 95 per cent of its costs. The improvements achieved would not have been possible without well-developed medical leadership, and staff having the skills in quality improvement methods acquired through the Advanced Training Programme. This programme draws heavily on Deming's approach to quality improvement described earlier, and adapted in Intermountain by Brent James.

Reflecting on this work, James and his colleague Savitz (2011) argue that there is scope to reduce costs by improving clinical outcomes. This requires a commitment to what they term **'organised care'** in which improvements are informed by rich clinical and financial data, led by clinicians themselves in partnership with researchers. Organised care is care that is managed and that reduces waste and unwarranted variations in clinical practice patterns. Other integrated delivery systems beyond Intermountain – such as Kaiser Permanente and Geisinger Health System – have demonstrated similar results.

As standardisation focuses first and foremost on clinical practice, it is essential to engage physicians and other clinicians in this work (Appleby *et al* 2010). Clinical leadership, underpinned by a culture of peer review and peer pressure, is especially important in professional bureaucracies like hospitals (to use Mintzberg's language) because of the autonomy of frontline clinical teams, and the challenge of disconnected hierarchies. Within these teams, the influence of respected peers is often far more important than the power of those in formal positions of authority. This illustrates the influence of collegial controls rather than hierarchical directives in changing professional practices, again highlighting the potential role of academic health science networks (AHSNs) in supporting change and improvement through collaborative working.

The experience of Intermountain and other systems underpins the case made by Swensen and colleagues for health care delivery to move from cottage industry to post-industrial care, described as 'combining the three elements of standardizing care, measuring performance, and transparent reporting' (Swensen *et al* 2010). This argument draws on the work of the Institute of Medicine (IOM), the Institute for Healthcare Improvement (IHI), Intermountain Healthcare and many others to propose a fundamental shift in how care is delivered. Given the provenance of this work on the other side of the Atlantic, it is not surprising that the advocates of organised care and post-industrial care do not argue for government to lead this shift. It is, however, telling that they argue for professional leadership rather than market forces as the best means of spreading what is already happening in high-performing organisations.

8 The role of patients

Many of the examples of high-performing health care organisations described earlier focused their improvement efforts on putting patients first (as in the case of the Virginia Mason Medical Center) and delivering improved outcomes for patients and citizens (evident in Jönköping County Council's creation of the fictional patient 'Esther' to guide specific changes). Other well-known international examples include the Cincinnati Children's Hospital, which uses patient- and family-centred rounds to put the needs of patients first. It is widely recognised as a centre of excellence in the care of children, and consistently receives a high ranking in US News and World Report ratings.

Salford Royal NHS Foundation Trust's improvement journey also illustrates the benefits of putting patients first; using charts above hospital beds enables patients and their relatives to make their views known in relation to the treatment and care being received. The trust also provides transparent reporting on its performance by displaying information about the quality of care on each ward using a colour-coding system. This includes information about required and actual staffing levels. All of these actions contribute to its high ratings in patient surveys.

In our analysis of the case for fundamental change in models of care, we identified enhancing the role of patients and users in the care team as one of the innovations needed to make a reality of new approaches to the delivery of care (Ham *et al* 2012). This includes experience-based co-design of care and co-production between patients and providers. The latter encompasses the systematic use of care planning, and supporting patients to play a bigger part in their own care as expert patients. The increasing prevalence of long-term conditions underlines the importance of supported self-care.

Shared decision-making between patients and those providing their care is another way in which the needs of patients can be put first. Mulley and colleagues describe the 'silent misdiagnosis' that occurs when patient preferences about treatment options are not elicited and acted on. They make a compelling case for doctors to have more and better information about what patients truly want, and for patients to have more and better information about options, outcomes and evidence (Mulley *et al* 2012). This is beginning to happen in some areas of care, but there is much more potential to involve patients – and their carers where appropriate – as partners in treatment decisions.

Self-directed care enables patients and users to take more control over their care and the services and support they need. Originally developed in social care through direct payments, self-directed care has been extended to health care through the use of individual budgets and personal health budgets. Evaluations have shown generally positive results in delivering care that is more personalised and customised, while also highlighting that such budgets may not be appropriate for all users and patients (Davidson *et al* 2012). The planned roll-out of personal health budgets from 2014 is a sign that this is an idea whose time has come.

One of the reasons why self-directed care may not be appropriate for all people is that patients often have very different motivations and capacities to play a bigger part in the design and delivery of care, including in decisions about their own health and wellbeing. Hibbard's work shows that highly activated patients understand their role in the care process and feel capable of fulfilling that role. Individuals with long-term conditions who are more activated are increasingly likely to engage in positive health behaviours and to self-manage their health conditions more effectively. The Patient Activation Measure is an established way of understanding the motivations of different people and its results can be used to offer appropriate support, which may lead to more appropriate use of services and help in tackling health inequalities (Hibbard and Gilburt 2014).

Looking to the future, information and communication technologies have the potential to revolutionise patients' and users' experiences. This can be seen in other health care systems that are already making use of these technologies to transform how patients communicate with providers. Integrated delivery systems such as Kaiser Permanente and Group Health, for example, have invested in comprehensive health information systems that enable their members to access medical records and test results online, order repeat prescriptions, make appointments, and email doctors and other providers. Members are also encouraged to use the telephone to seek advice. Group Health has harnessed these technologies alongside other innovations to redesign primary care provision, with face-to-face consultations used mainly for people with more complex needs who require more time with the doctor (Reid *et al* 2010).

In a paper prepared for The King's Fund, Coulter (2012) has argued that a strategic approach to patient engagement is needed, based on eight core elements:

- strong, committed senior leadership

- dedicated champions

- active engagement of patients and families

- clarity of goals

- focus on the workforce

- building staff capacity

- adequate resourcing of care delivery design

- performance measurement and feedback.

The challenge in transforming care is to put in place all these elements and overcome the barriers that hinder effective implementation.

Leading NHS reform and improvement

Leadership is the golden thread that runs through any analysis of NHS reform and improvement. This encompasses leadership by doctors and other clinicians, leadership by managers of NHS organisations, and leadership by politicians at a national level. In this penultimate section of the paper, we outline the kind of leadership that is needed to implement the transformation of care we have argued for.

Analysis undertaken by The King's Fund concludes that leadership in NHS organisations needs to be collective and distributed rather than left to a few individuals at the top of these organisations (The King's Fund 2011). The involvement of doctors, nurses and other clinicians in leadership roles is also essential, particularly in the clinical microsystems that comprise the basic building blocks of hospitals and other health care providers. Organisations in which skilled clinical leaders work with experienced managers can draw on different sources of expertise as they strive to achieve higher standards of performance. One of the most important roles of leaders is to develop the cultures that are conducive to the delivery of high-quality patient-centred care, as described in a recent study of the NHS (Dixon-Woods *et al* 2013).

Research has shown that there is a close correlation between staff satisfaction and the patient experience (Sizmur 2013). Patients receive better care when it is delivered by staff working in teams that are well led, have clear objectives, and where staff report that they have the time and resources to care to the best of their abilities. This highlights the critical role of team leaders, often experienced nurses, who develop the climate in which patients are treated with dignity and respect, and motivate their colleagues to do the same (Maben *et al* 2012). The work of West and others provides compelling evidence of the influence of staff engagement on organisational performance, and the role of leaders in promoting engagement. It shows that staff perform better when they are valued, supported, and respected, and have trust in their leaders (West *et al* 2011).

Leadership by politicians exerts an important influence, and this can be for ill or for good. We have argued elsewhere that today's political class typically lacks experience outside politics (Ham 2009). This means that health secretaries find themselves leading one of the biggest and most complex organisations in the Western world, with little if any understanding of how to discharge this responsibility effectively. Hardly surprising, therefore, that their record is distinctly mixed and often criticised. If medical practice is guided by a commitment to 'first do no harm', then political stewardship of the NHS might follow the same precept.

One of the consequences of rapid turnover among politicians and short-term horizons is lack of consistency and a tendency towards hyperactivity (Leatherman and Sutherland 2008). This militates against the commitment seen in high-performing organisations, which have a long-term vision of improvement that is well communicated and understood. Policy and politics operate on different cycles, which results in short-term political initiatives getting in the way of the long-term policy commitments needed to deliver transformational change (Collins 2014). Another unfortunate tendency is for politicians to reorganise the NHS on a frequent basis. Inevitably, this distracts attention from the much more important issues of quality improvement and service transformation.

An important lesson from high-performing organisations and the experience of the Veterans Health Administration (VA) is the need for alignment of goals and leadership at different levels, and coherence in the approach taken to improvement across the NHS. By this, we mean the need for system-wide goals to be communicated, understood and embraced by organisational and microsystem leaders. The challenge is how to achieve alignment in such a large and complex system as the NHS. Again, this underlines the critical role of national leaders – politicians and others – in creating a coherent national framework to enable those running local NHS organisations and services to bring about change at scale and pace. This includes providing the resources to support organisational and microsystem leaders to make improvements from within.

The experience of the VA points to the need to support leaders at all levels to take on new roles. Radical devolution of decision-making within the VA after years of centralised control created challenges of making the new operating structure and performance management approach work effectively. If the NHS is going to move in the same direction, then it must invest in leadership and organisational development to ensure that the right people are appointed with the appropriate skills. There is also a need to provide expertise on quality improvement methods, while not repeating the mistakes made with the NHS Modernisation Agency of over-centralising this expertise.

Both leadership development and training in quality improvement need to be priorities for NHS organisations themselves rather than being outsourced to national agencies. Vacancies in senior leadership positions in NHS organisations are an indication of the failure of recent approaches to leadership development in the NHS, including the Top Leaders programme, which was intended to increase the supply of qualified people for these positions. NHS organisations may need external support to strengthen leadership and redesign models of care, but this is best provided by agencies with an established track record in these areas.

Most of the resources currently used by the NHS Leadership Academy and NHS Improving Quality would be better deployed by NHS organisations themselves deciding how best to meet their needs. This might include collaborating to share resources and expertise, as is happening in some regions of England where leadership development and quality improvement are being supported through agencies funded on a subscription basis by NHS organisations themselves. In other areas, larger NHS organisations have developed in-house expertise of the kind found in high-performing organisations in other countries. Any national agencies should be small and expert, focusing only on those activities that cannot better be done at a local or regional level.

10 Where next for NHS reform?

In this final section, we draw together the main themes of the paper and elicit the implications for NHS reform in future. As noted at the outset, the focus is on what needs to be done to implement new models of care in the medium and longer term, rather than how to tackle the more immediate financial and service pressures facing the NHS.

Embrace complementary approaches to reform

The evidence and examples discussed in this paper present a major challenge to the dominant approaches to NHS reform over the past 20 years. Leaders of the NHS need to pursue complementary approaches in which politicians focus on steering the NHS towards the new models of care that are required, leaving the leaders of local NHS organisations to make change happen on the ground. Much more emphasis should be placed on bringing about improvement and change from within, and less emphasis on the use of external stimuli. Leaders need to align incentives, use information, encourage innovation, and pay more attention to the physiology of the system than to its anatomy. This includes removing the barriers to implementing new models of care and creating a permissive environment conducive to delivering the transformations in care that are needed.

A recurring theme has been the importance of fostering commitment rather than compliance within NHS organisations to bring about improvement and change. This means tapping into the intrinsic motivation of staff to do a good job, and relying less on extrinsic motivation, which, at its worst, can descend into fear and risk aversion. There is an important distinction here between regulated trust and real trust (Reeves and Smith 2006) – the latter being jeopardised by over-reliance on regulation and inspection by external agencies, as well as by targets and performance management. Reeves and Smith argue that 'over-regulating professionals can erode the foundations of their work' (p 5) and suggest that self-regulation and peer regulation are likely to be more effective than regulation from the outside.

Demarcate the role of politicians

Developing commitment rather than compliance depends on leaders of NHS organisations shrugging off the shackles of learned helplessness and recognising the role they have in leading transformational change. A new settlement is needed in which the strategic role of politicians is clearly demarcated to provide local leaders with the space and opportunity to innovate in the development of new models of care and the management of their services. Politicians have a key role in determining the level of funding that is required and can be afforded and in establishing priorities and objectives for the NHS through the Mandate. They must also be accountable to parliament for the overall performance of the NHS and how well its budget is used in their role as stewards of the system. But adapting Aneurin Bevan's dictum, the time has come for the sound of falling bedpans to stop reverberating around the Palace of Westminster and to locate accountability for operational issues where it properly belongs.

In demarcating the role of politicians we must learn from the experience of the 2012 Act, which sought to do precisely this. The provisions of the Act designed to limit detailed intervention by politicians have not only had little effect but also have been implemented in a context in which the Health Secretary's intervention in operational issues is greater than ever before (Campbell 2014b). This has been confirmed in a recent stakeholder audit conducted for the Department of Health by Ipsos MORI in which stakeholders reported that the Department's grip on the operational management of the NHS was tighter than expected (Iacobucci 2014). The centralising tendencies of the Westminster and Whitehall system, and expectations about accountability for the performance of public services, play a major part in this and make it difficult for well-intentioned initiatives designed to change how the NHS is managed to be carried through in practice. Also important are the working styles of ministers, with some politicians much more inclined to be activist and interventionist than others.

An analysis by the Institute for Government (IfG) of the challenges involved in reconciling ministerial accountability with decentralisation of public services argues that it is essential to clarify exactly what ministers are and are not responsible for (Moyes *et al* 2011). This includes developing an accountability map in which the implications for parliamentary oversight are set out. To counter the tendency to default back up the line, the IfG also argues that the statutory framework distributing powers within decentralised services should specify clearly where accountability resides. This is particularly important in relation to how operational failures are handled, as in the case of Mid Staffordshire NHS Foundation Trust, where public and political concerns may result in ministers feeling compelled to act even in a decentralised system.

Strengthening parliamentary oversight of decentralised public bodies like foundation trusts is one of the proposals advanced by IfG for ensuring that MPs and peers are able to scrutinise operational failures of this kind. Much the same applies to oversight of arm's length bodies such as the Care Quality Commission and Monitor given their role in inspecting and regulating the performance of NHS organisations. By allocating accountability for performance to those bodies best placed to discharge that accountability, it ought to be possible to both free up NHS organisations from inappropriate performance management and ensure that the public through parliament is enforcing accountability within the NHS in an effective manner.

Demarcating the role of politicians does not mean abandoning a role for ministers and national bodies in leading the NHS. Complementary approaches to reform require NHS England to set the direction for the NHS within the framework of the Mandate and to work with other national bodies to lend support to NHS organisations when they are in difficulty and to intervene to address performance concerns when necessary. As this happens, there needs to be greater consistency in the approach taken at a national level than has been the case in recent times both in the focus on developing new models of care and in improving patient safety and quality of care. This requires close collaboration and collective leadership by NHS England, the Care Quality Commission, Monitor, the NHS Trust Development Authority and other national bodies.

The point to emphasise is that the centre in its various forms needs to be more strategic and coherent, with politicians taking accountability for the performance of the NHS as a whole and being clear that it is not their role to become involved in operational matters. The early experiences of foundation trusts suggest this is not an impossible ambition (Moyes *et al* 2011) but it does depend on both ministers and parliament being committed to working in this way and not defaulting to old habits when operational failures and similar difficulties arise. Far from reducing accountability within the NHS, the approach set out here would help to strengthen it by establishing greater clarity on who is accountable for what, with the added benefit of freeing up NHS organisations to take full responsibility for the provision and improvement of services, with the framework set nationally.

Promote transparency

Another way of avoiding harmful intervention by politicians is to make much greater use of transparency based on the collection and open reporting of data on performance, drawing on the experience of star ratings and annual health checks in the 2000s. More recently, increasing effort has gone into collecting and publishing data about the outcomes of specialists in different areas of medicine. The examples given in this report of experience in other countries suggest that, used well, transparent reporting of information on performance has the potential to stimulate improvements in care by encouraging NHS leaders to investigate the reasons for discrepancies between the performance of their organisations and that of others, as they will be keen to avoid the reputational damage that comes from publicly reported poor performance.

Enable devolution

Transparency also requires that there is greater devolution within the NHS, learning from the experience of foundation trusts. The intention of the previous Labour government to devolve decision-making and accountability to foundation trusts was stymied by the compromise that accompanied their inception. Specifically, concerns within the Treasury about the risks of privatisation of NHS services meant that foundation trusts' freedoms were constrained. Their resulting semi-independent status means that today, they are as closely regulated as NHS trusts, with accountability to Monitor and the CQC being stronger than ever.

As a consequence, the promised freedoms of foundation trusts have not materialised, and their leaders often look up to the regulators rather than out to the communities they serve. This contrasts with the social enterprises formed when primary care trusts were required to relinquish control over the provision of community services. In some parts of England, these services are managed by community interest companies owned and run by staff. A forthcoming review of staff engagement in the NHS (Ham 2014) found that the leaders in these organisations feel a strong sense of accountability to staff as co-owners and to their communities. Less of their time is spent looking up to regulators and performance managers, creating more opportunity for leaders to innovate and improve care.

Drawing on this experience, the review argued that providers of NHS services should operate with presumed autonomy, and that the degree of regulation should be in proportion to organisational performance. This means fulfilling the ambitions that accompanied the creation of foundation trusts by removing the barriers to their autonomy and actively encouraging greater diversity of provider models, learning from the promising early experiences of many of the social enterprises providing NHS services. Whether working in foundation trusts or social enterprises, leaders need to have the time and space to engage staff in improving the quality and safety of the care they deliver and developing models of care appropriate to changing population needs. This will not happen if they are required to meet excessive demands of regulators and performance managers in a system that remains overly centralised at best and disempowering at worst.

Be realistic about inspection and regulation

There needs to be much greater realism about what inspection and regulation can contribute alongside other approaches to ensuring that care is safe and of a high standard. We have argued that there are three lines of defence in protecting patients from harm: the frontline teams delivering care, the boards leading NHS organisations, and inspectors and regulators – in that order. Inspection can only be effective if frontline teams and NHS boards are fully engaged in delivering the highest possible standards of care within available resources. The challenge for the CQC is to use its powers to facilitate reform from within, by supporting organisations to improve and avoiding the risks highlighted by Reeves and Smith (2006).

Alongside inspection, expert support should be available to organisations in difficulty, as in the work of agencies like the Emergency Care Intensive Support Team (ECIST), which visits organisations struggling to improve their urgent and emergency care to provide advice on how they can do better. A case can be made for the creation of additional teams to offer expert support to the NHS in other areas of care. The work of ECIST illustrates Gawande's insight, referred to earlier, on the role of person-to-person communication in spreading innovation.

See competition as one means to improve care rather than a guiding principle

The contribution of competition and choice to service transformation remains the most contentious aspect of NHS reform. The King's Fund has argued consistently that competition and choice do have a role to play, but should be used as just one means to improve care rather than being a guiding principle. The challenge is to learn from previous attempts to introduce competition into the NHS and why these have had modest impact at best. As Smith, Le Grand and others have noted, the design of the market needs careful thought, and effective implementation requires considerable managerial skills. Design questions include how providers should be organised to deliver beneficial results. Even then, it is important to take into account the transaction costs of the market and the likelihood of instability (Smith 2009).

It is also important to recognise the risk of the NHS embracing the 'wrong kind of competition', to borrow a phrase coined by Michael Porter and Elisabeth Teisberg in a different context (2006). By this, they mean competition that results in cost-shifting, attempts to capture patients and restrict choice, and competition that increases bargaining power. In its place, Porter and Teisberg make the case for value-based competition in which integrated practice units bring together the expertise needed to address a medical condition over the cycle of care, and incentives are used to reward value.

Support integration of care

Stimulating competition between integrated providers as Porter and Teisberg propose is one way of avoiding the risks of fragmentation that arise when markets are used in health care. Their arguments find echoes in the insights of Christensen and colleagues, who also contend that competition between integrated systems is the most promising way of promoting worthwhile innovations in care (Christensen *et al* 2009). This is because within integrated systems there is greater alignment of incentives in the way in which doctors and hospitals are paid and care is organised. Many of these systems are rewarded for keeping people healthy rather than simply treating illness, and they benefit when they provide services in outpatient and community settings instead of in hospitals.

The experience of the Veterans Health Administration (VA) lends strong support to these arguments and is especially relevant to the challenges facing the NHS in transforming models of care because of the shift from care provided in hospitals to care delivered in other settings. One of the lessons that can be drawn from its experience and that of other, well-established integrated systems such as Kaiser

Permanente and Group Health is that commissioning is a strategic function that brings the focus on how to fund and plan care. This is quite different from the fragmented and diffuse nature of commissioning in the English NHS – not to mention its constant restructuring – and suggests, at a minimum, the need to review how the commissioning function is organised and resourced in future.

The experience of these systems shows that benefits arise when providers are integrated and commissioning is seen as a strategic function in which scarce expertise is concentrated. These benefits occur through clinical and service integration rather than organisational integration (Curry and Ham 2010), indicating that effort needs to be put primarily into the development of alliances and networks between providers rather than mergers. Integrated systems represent one promising answer to the question posed above about how providers should be organised to deliver beneficial results through competition.

Strategic commissioning could also play an important part in reshaping the provision of specialist services in England. NHS England has responsibility for commissioning these services and could use its leverage to bring about the concentration of specialist services that will deliver better outcomes for patients in some areas of care. This could be instrumental in implementing long-overdue changes, not only in the location of specialist services but also in the provision of other hospital services that would benefit from co-location. The accountability of commissioners to the Health Secretary for delivery of the Mandate is another way of ensuring effective oversight of the use of NHS funding.

Promote collaboration

A closely related point is the need to encourage much greater collaboration between NHS organisations as a way of facilitating innovations in care and the spread of best practice. Academic health science networks (AHSNs) are beginning to work in this way in some areas, illustrating the opportunities to move away from improvements in care being driven mainly through the hierarchy, inspection or the market, to improvements occurring through collaboration between NHS organisations. The improvements in stroke care brought about in London show the benefits of this kind of collaboration. Networks and collaboration offer one way of spreading success and innovation, hence the interest currently being shown in chains of providers.

We argued in a previous report that AHSNs could lead the development of new models of care in London by grouping together providers in different areas under the leadership of the most able and experienced managers and clinicians (Ham *et al* 2013). As in the VA, AHSN leaders would be allocated a capitated budget by a London-wide strategic commissioner and would be held to account for the delivery of agreed outcomes. Network leaders would be empowered to work with foundation trusts and NHS trusts to bring about improvements in how care is delivered, learning from the changes to stroke care already implemented, and focusing on service change rather than structural change.

One of the risks in strengthening the role of AHSNs in this way is that they would evolve into geographical monopolies with few incentives to deliver high-quality care. To avoid this risk, and again drawing on the experience of the VA, AHSNs would be held to account for their performance by the strategic commissioner. Public reporting of performance data would help to stimulate AHSN leaders to compete with each other in a form of benchmarking or yardstick competition. Collaboration and competition would in this way go hand in hand.

Strengthen leadership and develop skills for improvement

Much more needs to be done to develop leaders and build capabilities for improvement at all levels. High-performing organisations invest heavily in in-house training and development for staff to equip them with the skills required to enable improvement to occur from within, supplemented by a commitment to learn from other organisations within health care and in other sectors. These organisations illustrate that change usually results from a sustained effort over time to which many people contribute. Bringing about this change requires persistence and hard work, and should not be seen as an easy alternative to the approaches that have dominated NHS reform in England recently.

Leaders of NHS organisations will need support to work in the way that is required to deliver improvements from within. This includes moving on from the dominant pacesetting style of top NHS leaders to embrace a wider repertoire of approaches to work towards the organisational development cultures that are characteristic of high-performing organisations and systems or networks (Jacobs *et al* 2013). The examples described earlier illustrate the importance of leaders who engage staff and other partners, and commit to change over the long haul. They also show that these leaders make a deep personal commitment to embracing change, leading by example alongside their colleagues. Developing stronger capabilities in system leadership, as opposed to organisational leadership, is particularly important. Much greater leadership continuity will be needed in NHS organisations to support new styles of leadership, with a focus on the development of leaders at all levels.

Commit to continuous improvement over the longer term

Implicit in the approach we are advocating is an acknowledgement that change in professional bureaucracies like hospitals depends much less on bold strokes and big gestures by politicians than on engaging doctors, nurses and other staff in continuous quality improvement over the longer term (Ham 2003). As Mintzberg (1979) observed many years ago, this is most likely to occur when these organisations develop leaders from the professions providing care, and support them to work with their peers to make change happen, as Lord Darzi advocated in the final report of the NHS next stage review (Department of Health 2008). This, of course, is precisely what can be seen in high-performing health care organisations, where improvement occurs through the aggregation of marginal gains.

These gains do not occur by accident. They are a consequence of intentional actions by leaders at many levels, focused on measuring and tackling variations in performance, engaging staff in reducing variations and eliminating waste, and systematically applying quality improvement methods. Spear's research into how this has been done in what he terms 'high-velocity organisations' in different sectors, including health care, contends that the particular method used is less important than how it is used (Spear 2010). Competitive advantage derives from recognising the need to solve problems in real time and creating opportunities for learning, not just from the rigour and discipline of the method itself. The experience of Salford Royal NHS Foundation Trust illustrates how this has been done in an English context.

Focus on organisations and networks

Spear uses the experience of the Virginia Mason Medical Center to illustrate his thesis. His arguments are echoed in Bohmer's analysis of what needs to be done to manage care to deliver improved performance (Bohmer 2009). Using the experience of Intermountain Healthcare and other high-performing organisations, Bohmer describes the characteristics of a learning system involving improvement methods, measurement and feedback, and learning from practice. Crucially, it requires a focus on what organisations themselves can do to improve their operating systems rather than what can be done by legislators or reformers operating at several steps removed from where care is delivered.

The fundamental shift we are arguing for requires a much stronger focus than hitherto on bringing about improvement and change **from within organisations and networks of care** as the route to system-wide transformation. The systems that inherit the future will be those that understand the limits on change led solely from the top down, and redouble their efforts to build leadership and quality improvement capabilities from the bottom up. They will be skilful in adapting the complementary approaches to reform described in this paper, in which national leadership is combined with devolution, collaboration with competition, and innovation with standardisation.

This is a difficult message to act on because the NHS remains one of the most centralised systems in the world, and path dependency in health care often frustrates the efforts of reformers to move away from established approaches. But move away they must if the mistakes of the past are to be avoided and improvement is to be put on a sustainable footing.

References

Appleby J, Galea A, Murray R (2014). *The NHS productivity challenge: experience from the front line.* London: The King's Fund. Available at: www.kingsfund.org.uk/publications/nhs-productivity-challenge (accessed on 2 May 2014).

Appleby J, Ham C, Imison C, Jennings M (2010). *Improving NHS productivity: more with the same not more of the same.* London: The King's Fund. Available at: www.kingsfund.org.uk/publications/improving-nhs-productivity (accessed on 14 May 2014).

Asch S, McGlynn E, Hogan M, Hayward R, Shekelle P, Rubenstein L, Keesey J, Adams J, Kerr EA (2004). 'Comparison of quality of care for patients in the Veterans Health Administration and patients in a national sample'. *Annals of Internal Medicine*, vol 141, no 12, pp 938–45. Available at: http://annals.org/issues.aspx (accessed on 14 May 2014).

Baker GR, MacIntosh-Murray A, Porcellato C, Dionne L, Stelmacovich K, Born K (2008). *High performing healthcare systems: delivering quality by design.* Toronto, ON: Longwoods Publishing.

Barber M (2008). *Instruction to deliver: fighting to transform Britain's public services.* London: Methuen.

Bate P, Mendel P, Robert G (2008). *Organizing for quality: the improvement journeys of leading hospitals in Europe and the United States.* Abingdon: Radcliffe.

Bevan G (2011). 'Regulation and system management' in Mays N, Dixon A, Jones L (eds), *Understanding New Labour's market reforms of the English NHS*, pp 89–111. London: The King's Fund.

Bevan G, Hood C (2006). 'Have targets improved performance in the English NHS?' *British Medical Journal*, vol 332, no 7538, pp 419–22.

Bevan G, Karanikolos M, Exley J, Nolte E, Connolly S, Mays N (2014). *The four health systems of the United Kingdom: how do they compare?* London: The Health Foundation and The Nuffield Trust. Available at: www.nuffieldtrust.org.uk/sites/files/nuffield/140411_four_countries_health_systems_full_report.pdf (accessed on 30 April 2014).

Bevan H, Ham C, Plsek P (2008). *The next leg of the journey: how do we make High Quality Care for All a reality?* London: NHS Institute. Available at: www.institute.nhs.uk/news/quality_and_value/ (accessed on 14 May 2014).

Bohmer R (2009). *Designing care: aligning the nature and management of health care.* Cambridge: Harvard Business Press.

Buchanan D, Fitzgerald L, Ketley D (2007). *The sustainability and spread of organisational change.* Abingdon: Routledge.

Cabinet Office (2006). *The UK Government's approach to public service reform: a discussion paper.* Pamphlet prepared by the Prime Minister's Strategy Unit in support of the conference '21st Century Public Services – Putting People First', London, 6 June 2006. Available at: http://webarchive. nationalarchives.gov.uk/20070701080507/cabinetoffice.gov.uk/strategy/downloads/work_areas/ public_service_reform/sj_pamphlet.pdf (accessed on 14 May 2014).

Campbell D (2014a). 'Hunt's decision to cancel the NHS pay rise shows just how tight money is'. *The Guardian*, 13 March.

Campbell D (2014b). 'NHS boss Simon Stevens to base himself in London'. *The Guardian*, 28 March.

Chassin M, Loeb J (2013). 'High-reliability health care: getting there from here'. *The Milbank Quarterly*, vol 91, no 3, pp 459–90. Available at: http://onlinelibrary.wiley.com/doi/10.1111/1468-0009.12023/abstract (accessed on 14 May 2014).

Christensen C, Grossman J, Hwang J (2009). *The innovator's prescription: a disruptive solution for health care.* New York: McGraw-Hill.

Coiera E (2011). 'Why system inertia makes health reform so difficult'. *British Medical Journal*, vol 342, d3693.

Collins P (2014). 'A symptom of broken Britain is fixed at last'. *The Times*, 28 February.

Cooper Z, Gibbons S, Jones S, McGuire A (2011). 'Does hospital competition save lives? Evidence from the English NHS patient choice reforms'. *The Economic Journal*, vol 121, no 554, pp F228–F260. Available at: http://onlinelibrary.wiley.com/doi/10.1111/j.1468-0297.2011.02449.x/abstract (accessed on 14 May 2014).

Coulter A (2012). *Leadership for patient engagement.* London: The King's Fund. Available at: www.kingsfund.org.uk/publications/leadership-engagement-for-improvement-nhs (accessed on 14 May 2014).

Curry N, Ham C (2010). *Clinical and service integration: the route to improved outcomes.* London: The King's Fund. Available at: www.kingsfund.org.uk/publications/clinical-and-service-integration (accessed on 14 May 2014).

Davidson J, Baxter K, Glendinning C, Jones K, Forder J, Caiels J, Welch E, Windle K, Dolan P, King D (2012). *Personal health budgets: experiences and outcomes for budget holders at nine months. Fifth interim report.* Personal Health Budgets Evaluation. Available at: www.gov.uk/government/ publications/personal-health-budget-pilots-fifth-interim-evaluation-report (accessed on 14 May 2014).

Department of Health (2008). *High quality care for all: NHS next stage review final report*. London: Department of Health. Available at: www.gov.uk/government/publications/high-quality-care-for-all-nhs-next-stage-review-final-report (accessed on 14 May 2014).

Dixon A, Robertson R (2011). 'Patient choice of hospital' in Mays N, Dixon A, Jones L (eds), *Understanding New Labour's market reforms of the English NHS*, pp 52–65. London: The King's Fund.

Dixon-Woods M, Baker M, Charles J, Dawson J, Jerzembek G, Martin G, McCarthy I, McKee L, Minion J, Ozieranski P, Willars J, Wilkie P, West M (2013). 'Culture and behaviour in the English National Health Service: overview of lessons from a large multimethod study' [online]. *BMJ Quality & Safety*, 9 September. Available at: http://qualitysafety.bmj.com/content/early/2013/08/28/bmjqs-2013-001947.full (accessed on 19 May 2014).

Edwards N, Kornacki M, Silversin J (2002). 'Unhappy doctors: what are the causes and what can be done?' *British Medical Journal*, vol 324, no 7341, pp 835–8.

Gawande A (2013). 'Slow ideas'. *The New Yorker*, July 29.

Gaynor M, Moreno-Serra R, Propper C (2010). *Death by market power: reform, competition and patient outcomes in the National Health Service*. CMPO Working Paper Series No. 10/242. Bristol: Centre for Market and Public Organisation. Available at: www.bristol.ac.uk/cmpo/publications/papers/2010/wp242.pdf (accessed on 3 June 2013).

Gilburt H, Peck E, Ashton B, Edwards N, Naylor C (2014). *Service transformation: lessons from mental health*. London: The King's Fund. Available at: www.kingsfund.org.uk/publications/service-transformation (accessed on 14 May 2014).

Gomez J (2010). 'Setting new standard in reducing deaths from life-threatening blood infections'. Intermountain Healthcare press release. Available at: http://intermountainhealthcare.org/about/news/Pages/home.aspx?NewsID=408 (accessed on 23 April 2014).

Gregory S, Dixon A, Ham C (2012). *Health policy under the coalition government: a mid-term assessment*. London: The King's Fund. Available at: www.kingsfund.org.uk/publications/health-policy-under-coalition-government (accessed on 14 May 2014).

Ham C (2014). *Improving NHS care by engaging staff and devolving decision-making*. Report of the Review of Staff Engagement and Empowerment in the NHS. London: The King's Fund.

Ham C (2009). *Health policy in Britain*, 6th ed. Basingstoke: Palgrave Macmillan.

Ham C (2008). 'World class commissioning: a health policy chimera?' *Journal of Health Services Research & Policy*, vol 13, no 2, pp 116–21. Available at: http://hsr.sagepub.com/content/13/2.toc (accessed on 14 May 2014).

Ham C (2007). *When politics and markets collide: reforming the English National Health Service*. Birmingham: Health Services Management Centre, University of Birmingham.

Ham C (2003). 'Improving the performance of health services: the role of clinical leadership'. *The Lancet*. Published online 25 March. Available at: http://image.thelancet.com/extras/02art8342web.pdf (accessed on 25 April 2014).

Ham C (1999). 'Improving NHS performance: human behaviour and health policy'. *British Medical Journal*, vol 319, 7223, pp 1490–2.

Ham C, Dixon A, Brooke B (2012). *Transforming the delivery of health and social care: the case for fundamental change*. London: The King's Fund. Available at: www.kingsfund.org.uk/publications/transforming-delivery-health-and-social-care (accessed on 14 May 2014).

Ham C, Edwards N, Brooke B (2013). *Leading health care in London: time for a radical response*. London: The King's Fund. Available at: www.kingsfund.org.uk/publications/leading-health-care-london (accessed on 14 May 2014).

Harford T (2001). *Adapt: why success always starts with failure*. London: Little, Brown.

Hewitt P (2006). Speech by Rt Hon Patricia Hewitt MP, Secretary of State for Health, to the New Health Network, 7 November.

Hibbard J, Gilburt H (2014). *Supporting people to manage their health: an introduction to patient activation*. London: The King's Fund. Available at: www.kingsfund.org.uk/patientactivation (accessed on 14 May 2014).

Hunter RM, Davie C, Rudd A, Thompson A, Walker H, Thomson N, Mountford J, Schwamm L, Deanfield J, Thompson K, Dewan B, Mistry M, Quoraishi S, Morris S (2013). 'Impact on clinical and cost outcomes of a centralized approach to acute stroke care in London: a comparative effectiveness before and after model'. *PLoS One*, vol 8, no 8, e70420.

Iacobucci G (2014). 'Jeremy Hunt interferes too much in day to day running of NHS, stakeholders say'. *British Medical Journal*, vol 348, g2983.

Institute for Healthcare Improvement (2008). *Achieving the vision of excellence in quality: recommendations for the English NHS system of quality improvement*. Report commissioned by Ara Darzi. Cambridge, MA: Institute for Healthcare Improvement. Available at: www.ajustnhs.com/wp-content/uploads/2012/09/IHI-report.pdf (accessed on 25 April 2014).

Jacobs R, Mannion R, Davies H, Harrison S, Konteh F, Walshe K (2013). 'The relationship between organizational culture and performance in acute hospitals'. *Social Science & Medicine*, vol 76, no 1, pp 115–25.

James B, Savitz L (2011). 'How Intermountain trimmed health care costs through robust quality improvement efforts'. *Health Affairs (Millwood)*, vol 30, no 6, pp 1185–91. Available at: www.ncbi.nlm. nih.gov/pubmed/21596758 (accessed on 14 May 2014).

Jarman B (2012). 'When managers rule'. *British Medical Journal*, vol 345, e8239.

Joint Commission International (2008). *Quality oversight in England – findings, observations, and recommendations for a new model*. Report commissioned by Ara Darzi. Illinois: Joint Commission International. Available at: www.ajustnhs.com/wp-content/uploads/2012/09/JCI-Report.pdf (accessed on 23 April 2014).

Kelling G, Bratton W (1998). 'Declining crime rates: insiders' views of the New York City story'. *The Journal of Criminal Law and Criminology*, vol 88, no 4, pp 1217–31.

Kenney C (2010). *Transforming health care: Virginia Mason Medical Center's pursuit of the perfect patient experience*. Portland: Productivity Press.

Kizer K, Dudley RA (2009). 'Extreme makeover: transformation of the Veterans Health Administration'. *Annual Review of Public Health*, vol 30, pp 313–39.

Larsson S, Lawyer P, Garellick G, Lindahl B, Lundström M (2012). 'Use of 13 disease registries in 5 countries demonstrates the potential to use outcome data to improve health care's value'. *Health Affairs (Millwood)*, vol 31, no 1, pp 220–27. Available at: http://content.healthaffairs.org/content/31/1.toc (accessed on 14 May 2014).

Le Grand J, Mays N, Mulligan J-A (1998). *Learning from the NHS internal market: a review of the evidence*. London: The King's Fund.

Leatherman S, Sutherland K (2008). *The quest for quality in the NHS: refining the NHS reforms*. London: Nuffield Trust. Available at: www.nuffieldtrust.org.uk/publications/quest-quality-nhs-refining-nhs-reforms (accessed on 14 May 2014).

Maben J, Peccei R, Adams M, Robert G, Richardson A, Murrells T, Morrow E (2012). *Exploring the relationship between patients' experiences of care and the influence of staff motivation, affect and wellbeing*. London: National Institute for Health Research Service Delivery and Organisation Programme. Available at: www.nets.nihr.ac.uk/projects/hsdr/081819213 (accessed on 14 May 2014).

Mays N, Dixon A, Jones L (eds) (2011). *Understanding New Labour's market reforms of the English NHS*. London: The King's Fund.

McGlynn EA, Shekelle P, Hussey P (2008). *Developing, disseminating, and assessing standards in the National Health Service: an assessment of current status and opportunities for improvement*. Report commissioned by Ara Darzi on the NHS. California: RAND Corporation. Available at: www.ajustnhs.com/wp-content/uploads/2012/09/RAND-Report.pdf (accessed on 25 April 2014).

Mintzberg H (1979). *The structuring of organizations.* Englewood Cliffs: Prentice Hall.

Moyes W, Wood J, Clemence M (2011). *Nothing to do with me? Modernising ministerial accountability for decentralised public services.* London: Institute for Government. Available at: www.instituteforgovernment.org.uk/publications/nothing-do-me (accessed on 21 May 2014).

Mulley A, Trimble C, Elwyn G (2012). *Patients' preferences matter: stop the silent misdiagnosis.* London: The King's Fund. Available at: www.kingsfund.org.uk/publications/patients-preferences-matter (accessed on 14 May 2014).

Oliver A (2007). 'The Veterans Health Administration: an American success story?' *The Milbank Quarterly*, vol 85, no 1, pp 5–35.

Orsini JN (ed) (2013). *The essential Deming. Leadership principles from the father of quality.* New York: McGraw-Hill Professional.

Pettigrew A (1999). *The determinants of organizational performance: a review of literature – final report.* Coventry: University of Warwick. Available at: http://onlinelibrary.wiley.com/doi/10.1111/milq.2007.85.issue-1/issuetoc (accessed on 14 May 2014).

Pham HH, Ginsburg P, McKenzie K, Milstein A (2007). 'Redesigning care delivery in response to a high-performance network: the Virginia Mason Medical Center'. *Health Affairs (Millwood)*, vol 26, no 4, w532–w544. Available at: http://content.healthaffairs.org/content/26/4.toc (accessed on 14 May 2014).

Porter M, Teisberg E (2006). *Redefining health care: creating value-based competition on results.* Boston: Harvard Business School Press.

Propper C, Dixon J (2011). 'Competition between hospitals' in Mays N, Dixon A, Jones L (eds), *Understanding New Labour's market reforms of the English NHS*, pp 78–88. London: The King's Fund.

Reeves R, Smith E (2006). *Papering over the cracks? – rules, regulation and real trust.* London: The Work Foundation. Available at: www.theworkfoundation.com/Reports/109/Papering-over-the-cracks-rules-regulation-and-real-trust (accessed on 14 May 2014).

Reid R, Coleman K, Johnson E, Fishman P, Hsu C, Soman M, Trescott C, Erikson M, Larson E (2010). 'The Group Health medical home at year two: cost savings, higher patient satisfaction, and less burnout for providers'. *Health Affairs (Millwood)*, vol 29, no 5, pp 835–43. Available at: http://content.healthaffairs.org/content/29/5.toc (accessed on 14 May 2014).

Salford Royal NHS Foundation Trust (2013). *Annual report and accounts, 1 April 2012 to 31 March 2013*. Salford, Manchester: Salford Royal NHS Foundation Trust. Available at: www.srft.nhs.uk/media-centre/publications/annual-reports-and-reviews (accessed on 25 April 2014).

Seddon J (2008). *Systems thinking in the public sector: the failure of the reform regime... and a manifesto for a better way*. Axminster: Triarchy Press.

Sizmur S (2013). *The relationship between cancer patient experience and staff survey results*. Oxford: Picker Institute Europe. Available at: www.pickereurope.org/staff-patient-experience-link.html (accessed on 14 May 2014).

Smith M, Saunders R, Stuckhardt L, McGinnis JM (2013). *Best care at lower cost: the path to continuously learning health care in America*. Washington DC: Institute of Medicine.

Smith P (2009). 'Market mechanisms and the use of health care resources' in OECD, *Achieving better value for money in health care*, pp 53–77. OECD Health Policy Studies, OECD Publishing.

Spear S (2010). *The high-velocity edge: how market leaders leverage operational excellence to beat the competition*. New York: McGraw-Hill.

Swensen S, Meyer G, Nelson E, Hunt G Jr, Pryor D, Weissberg J, Kaplan G, Daley J, Yates G, Chassin M, James B, Berwick D (2010). 'Cottage industry to postindustrial care – the revolution in health care delivery'. *The New England Journal of Medicine*, vol 362, no 5, e12. Available at: www.nejm.org/doi/full/10.1056/NEJMp0911199 (accessed on 14 May 2014).

The King's Fund (2011). *The future of leadership and management in the NHS: no more heroes. The report of The King's Fund Commission on leadership and management in the NHS*. London: The King's Fund. Available at: www.kingsfund.org.uk/publications/future-leadership-and-management-nhs (accessed on 14 May 2014).

Timmins N, Gash T (2014). *Dying to improve: the demise of the Audit Commission and other improvement agencies*. London: Institute for Government. Available at: www.instituteforgovernment.org.uk/publications/dying-improve (accessed on 14 May 2014).

Timmins N, Ham C (2013). *The quest for integrated health and social care: a case study in Canterbury, New Zealand*. London: The King's Fund. Available at: www.kingsfund.org.uk/publications/quest-integrated-health-and-social-care (accessed on 14 May 2014).

Tuohy C (1999). *Accidental logics: the dynamics of change in the health care arena in the United States, Britain and Canada*. Oxford: Oxford University Press.

Walshe K (2003). *Regulating healthcare: a prescription for improvement?* Maidenhead: Open University Press.

West MA, Dawson JF, Admasachew L, Topakas A (2011). *NHS staff management and health service quality: results from the NHS staff survey and related data.* Report to the Department of Health. Available at: www.gov.uk/government/publications/nhs-staff-management-and-health-service-quality (accessed on 14 May 2014).

Young G (2000). *Transforming government: the revitalization of the Veterans Health Administration.* Arlington, VA: PricewaterhouseCoopers Endowment for the Business of Government.

About the author

Chris Ham took up his post as Chief Executive of The King's Fund in April 2010. He was Professor of Health Policy and Management at the University of Birmingham between 1992 and 2014 and Director of the Health Services Management Centre at the university between 1993 and 2000. From 2000 to 2004 he was seconded to the Department of Health, where he was Director of the Strategy Unit, working with ministers on NHS reform.

Chris has advised the World Health Organization and the World Bank and has served as a consultant on health care reform to governments in a number of countries. He is an honorary fellow of the Royal College of Physicians of London and of the Royal College of General Practitioners, and a companion of the Institute of Healthcare Management. He is a founder fellow of the Academy of Medical Sciences.

Chris was a governor and then a non-executive director of the Heart of England NHS Foundation Trust between 2007 and 2010. He has also served as a governor of the Canadian Health Services Research Foundation and the Health Foundation and as a member of the advisory board of the Institute of Health Services and Policy Research of the Canadian Institutes of Health Research.

Chris is the author of 20 books and numerous articles about health policy and management. He is currently emeritus professor at the University of Birmingham and an honorary professor at the London School of Hygiene & Tropical Medicine. He was awarded a CBE in 2004 and an honorary doctorate by the University of Kent in 2012. He was appointed Deputy Lieutenant of the West Midlands in 2013.

Acknowledgements

I would like to thank Beccy Ashton at The King's Fund for providing research assistance, and Laura Carter for helping to get the paper into the right format. Outside the Fund, helpful comments were sought and received from Ross Baker, Ian Dodge, Ken Kizer, Nick Mays, and Caroline Tuohy. I am indebted to colleagues within the Fund, including Jocelyn Cornwell, Catherine Foot, Rebecca Gray, Nicola Hartley, Candace Imison, Richard Murray, Patrick South, Katy Steward, Nick Timmins, and Michael West. Any errors and omissions are entirely my responsibility.

The King's Fund is an independent charity working to improve health and health care in England. We help to shape policy and practice through research and analysis; develop individuals, teams and organisations; promote understanding of the health and social care system; and bring people together to learn, share knowledge and debate. Our vision is that the best possible care is available to all.

www.kingsfund.org.uk   🐦 **@thekingsfund**

Published by
The King's Fund
11–13 Cavendish Square
London W1G 0AN
Tel: 020 7307 2568
Fax: 020 7307 2801

Email:
publications@kingsfund.org.uk

www.kingsfund.org.uk

© The King's Fund 2014

First published 2014 by
The King's Fund

Charity registration number:
1126980

All rights reserved, including
the right of reproduction in
whole or in part in any form

ISBN: 978 1 909029 32 3

A catalogue record for this
publication is available from
the British Library

Edited by Kathryn O'Neill

Typeset by Grasshopper
Design Company

Printed in the UK by
The King's Fund